Also by Nancy Bos

Singing 101: Vocal Basics and Fundamental Singing Skills
for All Styles and Abilities

Cantar 101: Principios vocales y destrezas fundamentales de canto para
todos los estilos y habilidades

Singing Through Change: Women's Voices in Midlife, Menopause, and
Beyond

Singer's Practice Plan, Log and Journal: A Planner for Singing Students

Available on Amazon or through StudioBos.com

THE TEEN GIRL'S SINGING GUIDE

Tips for Making Singing the Center of Your Life

Nancy Bos

Nancy Bos
Visit my website at nancybos.me

Printed in the United States of America

First Printing: Aug 2017
StudioBos Media

ISBN-13: 9781973409113

This book is dedicated to every teen girl who has studied voice with me. Your amazing lives and passion for music have inspired me for decades. Thank you for your trust and love.

My deep gratitude goes to Athena Williams for her wonderful characters living in this book, and to Stacey Miyahara for the fabulous cover.

Thank you to all of the people who contributed to the book: Dr. Diana Allan, Alexis O'Donahue, Valerie White Williams, and Meghan Moore.

Thank you to the many people who helped me with development, editing, and proofing, especially Samantha Bos, Lindsey Costlow, Dr. Julie Cross, Leora Schwitters, and Cynthia Vaughn.

CONTENTS

INTRODUCTION

There aren't many things in the world that are as personal as singing. I bet you knew that, right? If you love to sing you know how music makes you feel and how important it is. But there are lots things in life that seem more urgent. Every day there are a mess of responsibilities and assignments that come at you. All of those things make it hard to decide what is most important. And they make it hard to look at the big picture - there is so much little picture stuff in the way.

This book is here to help you learn more about how to make singing the center of your life. If you take time to sincerely focus while you read it, this book will help you make some big decisions and help you prioritize the little stuff.

Amelia

Sophia

Lizzie

Meradee

Let me introduce the four girls who will be on this journey with you. Amelia, Sophia, Lizzie, and Meradee. They are four very different girls thinking through this information in different ways. I think you'll enjoy getting to know them as you read.

In this book you'll be asked to think about what singing means to you and the people around you. We will talk about ways you might be feeling and work out a possible path for you to make singing a part of your life for as long as you want it to be.

Sometimes we let other things push music out of our lives, and we suffer for it. But other times singing can take on too big a role and pushes everything else away. We will talk about how to find a good balance.

We'll look at career options, voice study, and college decisions. We'll talk about performance anxiety, the discipline of practicing, and how to stay motivated. And we will talk about skill building in complementary areas like acting, music theory, and movement.

Every one of us has had to make decisions when we felt like we didn't have enough information. How the heck could any of us know if we've made the right decisions? It just isn't fair sometimes. This book aims to make it a little fairer - to give you the chance to make smart, well informed decisions.

Take the time to read the whole book through. If you want to reach out and connect with me or other people who are taking about these things, connect on Facebook, Instagram, and at NancyBos.net.

So now, are you ready to get started? Are you ready to ask some questions and find some answers? Then let's go!

PART 1: HOW IMPORTANT IS SINGING TO YOU?

Start with your heart. Close your eyes and look inside your heart. This will only take a minute - wait, don't close your eyes yet. Read this first.

Looking inside *your* heart means you ignore everyone else's opinions. At this moment it doesn't matter what any else thinks. This moment is about you.

When you look inside, ask yourself one simple question: "How important is singing to me?" After you feel you have that answer delivered from your heart to your brain, either say it out loud or write it down in this book, or both. I want it to travel from your heart, to your brain, outside of you (through speech and writing), and back in (through hearing and seeing).

Ready? Here we go...
"How important is singing to me?"

Did you say your answer out loud or write it down?

Your next step is to read the rest of this chapter. At the end you are going to write down more about what you are thinking. If you are worried about somebody reading what you write in this book then write it someplace else or make an audio recording. This is private stuff. Write it someplace where you might run across it in ten years. I love going back to see what young me wrote about, and I bet old you will like it too.

Five Perspectives On Singing And Singing Lessons

Most people can identify with one of five perspectives about singing. I've put them in levels or tiers, from "Meh, singing's cool but not that big of a deal." to "Singing is EVERYTHING! Sing or Die!"

Here is a list of the tiers:
- ❖ Meh, not that big of a deal.
- ❖ One of many life skills I'd like to learn.
- ❖ Important to me, my family, and community.
- ❖ Really, really important to me - singing will be part of my whole life.
- ❖ Sing or Die!

Meh, not that big of a deal

Let's start with "Meh, not that big of a deal." I'll keep it short. If you are looking forward to reading this book, then you are not "meh." But there are some people for whom singing is totally meh. What are you meh about? What things interest your friends but really don't mean anything to you? Here are two examples for me. I don't really care about learning motorcycle mechanics. If somebody offered me a free, three hour class on motorcycle mechanics would I take it? Probably. I love to learn and who knows, maybe some of the information would transfer and be useful in some other area of my life.

If someone offered me a three hour course in how to reprogram a plush pet robot - teaching them to follow commands, say what I want them to say, and wiggle their ears at just the right time - would I take it? No. My mind is not built to appreciate plush pet robot mechanics and programming, and I am sure it would not benefit me in the future. Do you agree with me, don't care about either thing, or think both sound cool? That's good - we need to all be different and have different motivations in order for this world to be interesting.

So what category do singing lessons fall into for the "meh" person - the motorcycle mechanics class or plush pet robot reprogramming?

That's easy - the one that would be ok and not boring. Because taking singing lessons will definitely and without a doubt transfer to skills in other areas. For example, I've had three students, all medical doctors, who took singing lessons so that they could become better public speakers and presenters, and to increase their vocal stamina so they could talk all day. Also, I've had students who are parents of babies and toddlers who've taken singing lessons so they could sing their baby to sleep or join in on singing toddler music without being self-conscious. Those are all people who are meh about singing lessons but still take them, and that's great!! It can only make their lives richer.

One of many life skills I'd like to learn

Next level is "One of many life skills I'd like to learn." This is an interesting group. Older people in this group say things like, "I've always wanted to sing but..." and "I can't sing." Let's take a look at this "I can't sing" statement. It is so harsh - so definite. "Can't" is a strong word. When I hear high schoolers say, "I can't sing" it is usually followed by "...yet" or "...but I want to" or "...very well." Those responses leave a door open for hope that with a little work "I can be a singer, too." But later in life the grown-ups seem to shut that door.

Can anyone learn to sing? Yes, pretty much anyone who can talk clearly can sing. Talking and singing are in separate parts of the brain, so I can't guarantee that the two skills are best buddies, but the vast majority of people can learn to sing well. Some people say they are tone deaf, but this is exceedingly rare. Maybe we could say "tone disadvantaged" but not tone deaf. If you can tell by listening if someone is asking a question versus making a statement, you are hearing the change in pitch. If other people can hear that change of pitch in your voice, then you have control over pitch. So it is just a matter of training to improve singing.

Perhaps the biggest issue for this group is whether it is worth the time and money to learn to sing. That's why some retirees who have some money finally take the plunge. For you, if you are not interested in spending three to five hours a week practicing then lessons aren't for you right now. If you have time for a little bit of singing, then taking choir (or chorus) at school would be a lot of fun. Choir is a great way to have singing as part of your life, to spend time with friends, and grow your brain. Just don't let that door close - keep the option open.

Important to me, my family, and community

There are some skills that can bring more joy to you than you can imagine, and the absence of that skill can cause more un-joy. Un-joy is a funny word but it encompasses everything that is the opposite of joy; dissatisfaction, anger, irritation, depression, self-doubt, misery... If not knowing how to sing well is causing you un-joy, then work on your voice.

> How much you invest - both in time and money - might be the biggest question.

Singing in a school choir would be mostly free but take at least five hours of your week. Singing in a show might cost more money and take up to ten hours per week. Perhaps you are in the very large camp of girls who would like to take weekly one-on-one singing lessons. If you do, your skills will grow quickly. Individual lessons are an efficient way to learn what you need to know quickly. Your teacher will expect you to practice every day, memorize songs, sing in recitals, and perhaps a contest or two. So you can see all of those new expectations will take time. If you have a season when you are less busy - like after soccer season, before cheer-leading starts, during the summer - propose to a teacher that you would like to take lessons for that limited time. Give it a shot for a few months, but be clear with the teacher that once the next big activity starts you'll need to take an extended break.

Individual singing lessons are definitely the most direct path to becoming a better singer. In over two decades of teaching, I am sure that every single student who has come through my studio - even if for just one lesson - has taken away tools they could use to be a better singer.

But if individual singing lessons are not a good option right now, and you've already got a choir or show, then you might be looking for that next step you can easily take to improve your singing. Luckily, there are great inexpensive options. My *Singing 101* book is written for you - for the person who wants to get better at singing! It is a short book packed with wisdom, exercises, and actions you can take on your own to improve your skills. It is best experienced in audiobook form from Audible.com, or you can find it on Amazon, and my website. You will also find links to lots of other bonus material on my website, NancyBos.net.

One free way to learn more is with teachers who have created YouTube instruction. Try to make sure the teacher is great. And for the best experience, look for a teacher who knows how to teach *you*. For YouTube content, avoid teachers working in a different genre and also guys teaching toward guys; stick with women who teach in your style. They are more likely to address things in a way that fits a girl's voice best. Three teachers who have great YouTube channels are:

Karyn O'Connor (Wingwise.com)
Valerie White Williams (VocalSplendor.com)
Cheryl Porter (CherylPorterMethod.com/)
Check out their websites and YouTube pages.

Really-really important to me - singing will be part of my whole life

This is great news - I understand your love of singing; how it frees your spirit, expands your mind, and involves your whole body. I have no doubt that you will be singing for your entire life and that is wonderful. One of the best gifts you can give yourself is to study singing while you are in middle school or high school. Why now? Because it will set the foundation of great technique early on. You will avoid un-joy (see the previous section), and you'll enjoy giving hours each week to singing and studying. On top of the singing you are already doing, you will need to study songs in various genres and languages, work on sight reading and theory, and practice technique improvements every day. The usual way to do those things is in weekly voice lessons. But it is possible, if you are highly motivated and driven, to study those things on your own. Or contact me about a hybrid approach; I'll give you assignments and see you for an on-line live check-in/lesson once per month.

Two advantages of studying with a local teacher are networking and community. You will find community in the voice studio - students often don't meet each other during weekly lessons, but instead get to know each other at recitals and contests. But what if you don't have time or money for singing lessons right now? Then I suggest you take advantage of the resources listed in the previous tier.

Make the time and save the money for individual lessons in the near future. Carve out the time. If it means you have to quit something else, consider that as a strong possibility, but maybe you can get away without quitting. For instance, you might think you have to quit volleyball to take singing lessons. But take a good look at it - can't they be compatible? Is there one afternoon or evening a week that you don't have volleyball that you could take a lesson? Perhaps a Saturday morning? Good! But what about the practice? That's easy. You can practice when you are taking a shower, putting on make-up, driving to school. You can study lyrics at lunch, study technique while you wait for your toast, and listen to your songs while you walk to the bus. If singing is important to you, there is no better time to improve than now. Make the time, take the jump. You won't regret it.

Sing or Die!

If you have the "Sing or Die!" perspective, you are already in the school choir, musical, and probably the jazz choir too. You sing in a church or community choir, and you participate in a community or church youth theatre program. You might have a rock band, or busk (be a street performer) in a subway. Your mom has you sing for her friends. You've started an *a cappella* group, and you are president of the Music Club!

Does this sound like you? And are you considering a career in singing? Then timing is everything. The sooner you start singing lessons, the more competitive you will be for college auditions. The best college music programs are hard to get into - you have to become a special singer with a special résumé and excellent music skills. The most serious students in my studio - the ones you will be competing against for colleges - start individual voice lessons when they are 8 or 9 years old. By the time they are 18 they have 10 years of one-on-one lessons under their belts!

So get going - find that teacher and start voice lessons this week!

Write It Down

Now it's time to write it down
(Here or someplace secret)

What does your heart say now, after everything you've read about singing?

Are you a:
- ❖ Meh
- ❖ One of Many Skills
- ❖ Important to Me and People Around Me
- ❖ Really-Really Important to Me
- ❖ Sing or Die!

What Now?

Every action you take regarding singing from here on out depends on what you just wrote. And that's what this book is about; what the best things are to do and how to do them.

You aren't forced to stay in one of the *5 Perspectives.* You have every right to float between them or combine a couple. You are unique. Don't let words in a book tell you what to do. But do let this book tell you what you *can* do. Keep in mind what you wrote in the previous section and use it to help you decide on your action steps.

What Is the End Goal?

Knowing where you are heading makes a huge difference in the path you take. If you were in Houston and had to get to Boston, you'd want a map. But what if you didn't have a map? You'd be like, "I think I have to go northeast." And you'd take every road that went northeast. The problem is, you might end up anywhere from Charlotte, NC to Montreal, Quebec! Are you ok with ending up anywhere from Charlotte to Montreal? Yes? Great - close this book now and never look at it again. Would you like a map? Yes? Cool! Let's make a map for your singing by starting with your goal.

We started to figure out your goals with the *5 Perspectives*. Later in the book there is a big list of careers for you to consider. But I don't want you to decide right now what you are going to be doing when you are 25. Instead, get to the right *state*.

Ask yourself questions like:

- ❖ Do I want to live a professional performer's lifestyle (poor and humble but maybe someday not poor)?
- ❖ Do I love singing harmony more than anything?
- ❖ Do I love behind-the-scenes work?
- ❖ Do I love the spotlight?
- ❖ Is indie rock the path for me?

- Do I care what kind of singing I do?
- Am I crazy about voice science or medicine?
- Is opera the most amazing kind of singing?
- Is career or family more important to me?
- Is making costumes or sets the best part of a show?
- Is singing for worship the only important thing to me?
- Do I love to run the theater or company more than being in the show?
- Do I like helping or teaching people more than performing?
- Does singing in coffeehouses, restaurants, and summer festivals sound fun?

I think you can see that many of these questions do not point to standing under the white hot spotlight. The fact is, the percentage of the population that actually stands under that spotlight is minuscule, and competition is fierce. Even once somebody gets there, their peers will probably attack.

Let's super simplify this and act like there are three basic, really big, well-traveled paths to a life in singing. You already know what your heart wants. Now let's use your brain to pick a path. Read about these three goal/path combinations and see if one of them sounds like the best fit for you.

♦♦♦

Goal #1
I want to be a successful, full-time professional singer.
Path #1
Now might be the time to sing, perform, network, master an instrument, and post high quality videos and audio that you won't regret later. Once your regular fan base grows, build your mailing/subscriber list. Go to summer performance camps and go to workshops all year. Work hard on your DIY career and start now.

♦♦♦

Goal #2
I want to be a serious well-rounded musician.
Path #2
Study deliberately and with focus. Perform some. Build skills and network. Learn all you can.

♦♦♦

Goal #3
I love to sing but it's not everything.
Path #3
Sing for your own enjoyment and the enjoyment of your community. Consider also gaining skills in complementary interests, like business, audio engineering, video production, voice science, costume design, music therapy, and music ministry.

Brainstorming time

Based on the three paths, write down the number of the Goal/Path combo that speaks to you the loudest; 1, 2, or 3.

Now brainstorm all of the things you can think of that might make you happy with this path. On the next pages write career ideas, life/balance ideas, or how much of your life you want to devote to singing. Write down whatever the thought of this path makes you think or feel.

On this page and the next, write down career ideas, life ideas, or how much of your life you want to devote to singing. Write down whatever the thought of this path makes you think or feel.

The pages too big? Maybe you need more information first. Read on and you can come back to this later.

The pages aren't big enough? No problem - there are some blank pages at the end of the book.

Let's Go!

It's time to learn more about your journey. You sorta know what *state* you are headed toward, and there is still plenty of time to alter your course. The next section is about how to become a better singer - what things you should experience and know as you head down the road. It will help you understand the different areas of singing that a professional singer should master. Maybe you'll find some things in Part 2 that make you say, "No Way. I am not interested in that At All." That's fine! Knowing what you do and don't like about singing is exactly how you'll make smart decisions about what to do next.

PART 2: SKILLS FOR BECOMING A BETTER SINGER

There are three main areas for singers to focus on, all at the same time:

artistic expression

physical skills

and mental skills

This is the same as for a dancer or other athletic artist who studies style, technique, and methods.

How can you do that? With practice, reading, and skill building.

We will take a close look at different ways to build these skills (through individual voice lessons, choir, and shows). We will also look at studying how professional singers use technique and emotion. Some are good at it, some not so good. We'll look at how you can deliberately build the physical skills on your own. And some other topics we'll cover are: vocal health, best ways to practice, and what to do if you have performance anxiety.

As you can see, there are lots of things to learn and eventually master. This section helps you understand how to get a foundation in many of them.

Study Singing Through Voice Lessons

Taking voice lessons is super focused and active, not passive. It is like being in a sport and hiring the coach of your choice to guide you to being your best.

What are some of the things that any of us wants to get out of any new, big activity? We want:

- ❖ to be part of something meaningful to us
- ❖ to be where we can find friends
- ❖ to be at least a little bit good at it
- ❖ to be happy
- ❖ to be working toward our future goals
- ❖ to be smarter

And the good news is that studies show music lessons do make us smarter! Music students do better academically than non-music students. (Of course, if you skip doing your homework in order to practice, you won't actually have a brain-gain.) You can learn more about the benefits of music education at this site: www.pbs.org/parents/education/music-arts/the-benefits-of-music-education

Being part of something meaningful is huge. Some would say it is the meaning of life. Does going to your voice teacher's studio for 30 - 60 min. a week fulfill that meaning? Absolutely not. But it is part of the puzzle. Learning the best

technique in anything means that you will be able to rise above the process when you are performing the task. That's a little vague - let me give you an example. Have you ever seen a toddler learn to walk? It is heroic! They take a big risk of doing a face-plant every time they try. But something about being human calls us to learn to walk. And if we didn't learn the technique of walking, we would be so dissatisfied with life!

Another example is learning to skateboard. I have never learned to skateboard, and I have skateboard envy. I see girls on skateboards, flying down the road, hair flowing behind them.

Or grabbing air at the skate park and shouting for joy when they land a jump.

What an awesome feeling that must be! I want to feel that! The problem is, I don't have the technique. So I'm learning. I got a skateboard, and I practice. It is risky and sometimes embarrassing, but it will be worth it.

With singing, pretty much everybody can sing without lessons. But if you study singing by taking lessons, you get to learn the best technique, so you can transcend technique. You can get beyond being distracted by what you are bad at or good at - with hard work you will be good at all of it. The possibility to be really transformed and moved while singing is a goal you can achieve if you work on technique. In my teens and twenties I was too wrapped up in how I sounded, too insecure about what people thought of my singing.

But I am so grateful that I challenged myself, worked hard, and got past those hurdles. Thanks to putting in the time and work on my technique, I've gotten to belt out emotional, heartfelt songs in theaters and concert halls, and I've gotten to take flight with my voice into the rafters of European cathedrals and opera houses. It is an amazing feeling, and I wish it for you!

Aside from spiritual transformation someday, what else can you get out of singing lessons? How about confidence in singing right now? Have you ever gotten a comment about your singing from somebody who doesn't really know any more than you do, and that comment made you self-conscious or unsure? Or have you ever gotten advice from somebody who might know what they are talking about, but you don't know if it applies to you, like from an aunt who has taken lessons, or a choir director who is talking to your whole section? Or have you ever listened to a recording of your own voice and not liked it? Taking singing lessons can get you beyond all of that. Find a teacher who is a talented, qualified, singing expert who can guide you every step of the way. Then you can own your confidence and know that you deserve it.

The last piece we might want to get from lessons is community; we want to make friends and share the journey with others. Honestly, choirs and musical theater are great for that, and so is starting a band. But can you get community out of one-on-one singing lessons? With some teachers, yes, and with others, no. Some voice studios offer group classes, studio performances, and field trips to shows. Some studios don't do any of that. So if working with friends in voice lessons is important to you, make sure you consider that when picking a teacher.

The benefits of taking singing lessons are almost too many to list. And it is a life-long study; every famous singer you've ever heard never stopped learning. I've taught and talked to many older professional singers who are still studying technique and performance skills after decades in the business. And they all started somewhere with their first voice teacher showing them the way. You can join them in the big community of singers.

Options for Where to Study

There are three basic locations you can study voice. By far the most common is to go to a voice teacher's school or home-based studio. Alternatively, you might find a teacher who travels to your home. And a third and growing option is on-line lessons. Here is a good look at all three options so you can decide what is best for you. Oh, but there's  a fourth option that Beyonce took advantage of: have a very good voice teacher live in your house. Honestly, in the rare situation that your parents have a spare room to rent, this is a really cool idea.

Lessons at the Teacher's Studio

Most students go to a teacher's studio. This is usually the best choice if it is something you are able to do. I realize it isn't for everyone; maybe you don't have a way to get to lessons, or perhaps there are no singing teachers within miles. In those cases, you should look at the other two options. But here are a few points on the plus side of going to a teacher's studio:

- ❖ You won't be self-conscious about your family listening in. The studio should be private, and parents rarely sit in on their kid's lessons.
- ❖ It will be a professional environment, unlike your home. No dogs, birds, little sisters/brothers. Dinner won't be cooking in the next room and the piano will always be in tune (If these

problems exist in the teacher's studio, think twice about whether it is worth putting up with unprofessional conditions to study with this teacher).

- ❖ All of the music, sound system, computer, and piano will be right there - easy access to everything for an efficient experience.
- ❖ You'll meet other students coming and going.

Are there any disadvantages to going to a teacher's studio? There are two I can think of: you might depend on a ride or bus to get there, and it takes more of your time. However, you can use that time in the car or bus to study your music, so some people consider that a plus.

Lessons at Your House

Having a teacher come to you can be great if your house is set up for it. All the teacher needs is a keyboard and a quiet space away from distractions. The better quality the keyboard or piano, the better for the teacher. But any full-sized keyboard will actually do.

You might wonder why a teacher would come to you. It's really simple: because they don't have a place of their own to teach. That can mean the teacher lives in an apartment that wouldn't be good for teaching, or lives far from a population center so commutes in to teach. However, there is a big downside for the teacher - it takes them time to get from lesson to lesson. Expect the teacher to charge for the drive, adding to the cost of lessons. Also keep in mind that the teacher will not have access to all of their music, and your home might not be the optimal learning environment. However, there are some pluses for you:

- ❖ Zero commute for you
- ❖ Your family gets to hear your lesson
- ❖ You will never forget to bring your music

Lessons On the Internet

Do you wonder if online lessons on your are good idea?
To answer that question, I turned to Valerie White Williams. Valerie has been teaching and singing since long before I met her in the VocalistUsenet newsgroup (the earliest form of internet discussion groups) in 1993! We even sang together in an internet organized virtual recital on video tapes, with performers spanning the globe. There is nobody more qualified that I know of to talk to us about taking  lessons over the internet since Valerie has been deep in the internet since those early days.

NOTE: Valerie uses the words *virtual lessons* to represent all on-line one-on-one, live streaming apps which includes FaceTime, Zoom and others. Another option would be to call them "live online web based lessons." (LOWBL?)

◆◆◆

<u>Nancy</u>: Do virtual lessons really work as well as in-person lessons?

Valerie: Yes! I was skeptical at first. But then I was totally surprised with how easy it was for me to tune into my students, hear what is going on with their voices, and offer them instruction and feedback, just like in-person lessons. Since then, I've worked with students all over the world and I can honestly say they progress just as fast as my in-person students.

Nancy: What things are different about virtual lessons?

Valerie: Besides not having to go to your teacher's house or music studio, there really aren't many differences. First off, you don't have to spend time traveling to lessons. But if you are used to using your teacher's music, for virtual lessons you need to have the music and the accompaniment tracks you are working on available on your end.

Nancy: What are the benefits of virtual lessons?

Valerie: First off, you can take lessons with a teacher anywhere in the world! You are not limited to the teachers (or lack of them) in your local area. But the best thing about live virtual lessons is that web based platforms, like Zoom & FaceTime, use a split screen with a double mirror effect.

Singing into a mirror is one of the most beneficial things singers can do, yet it is so awkward! The double mirror effect on the

computer screen makes everything more comfortable and easy for your teacher to demonstrate and for you to clearly see what they are doing! It also creates great bonding since on-line lessons are more direct face-to-face in ways that might feel too creepy in real life.

Other benefits include the ease of recording lessons through add-on recording programs and the ability to warm up before and practice new things right away after the lesson.

Nancy: Are there any downsides of virtual lessons?

Valerie: There are only two downsides that I can think of. The first is that tech issues can happen. Sometimes the connection is bad and there can be a delay, but that is becoming less and less common as bandwidth is increasing. I've found that if the connection is bad, it's best to hang up and call again. That often fixes the issue.

The other downside is that most teachers cannot accompany their students in real time. If the connection is strong on both ends, it can sometimes work out but usually teachers and students need to take turns speaking, playing and/or singing. So when working on a song or vocal exercise, the teacher plays the exercise or vocal line at the piano and then you sing it back and so on, back and forth. Although this may seem like a drawback, it actually helps the students listen more carefully as they sing back what they hear. But when it comes to actually accompanying the students while they sing, it just doesn't work. Any accompaniment or backing track needs to be happening in the student's location. The students can then sing along to the accompaniment on their end so that the teacher can give feedback and suggestions.

Nancy: Do online lessons cost more?

Valerie: No. I charge the same as in-person lessons, and I think most teachers are the same.

Nancy: How do virtual lessons actually work? It sounds complicated.

Valerie: Here is what you need for live, web based lessons:

* **A computer, laptop or iPad or other large tablet.** Phones are too small to see well enough to really be effective.

* **A web cam.** I use a separate HD webcam through my laptop because it gives me better placement options as well as a better picture. But you can simply use the camera that comes with your tablet or laptop.

* **Internet with good bandwidth.** Streaming video is intense. Depending on your bandwidth, you might ask people who are sharing the connection with you at your home to stay off Netflix and YouTube while you have your lesson. Some people find the connection is best when using an ethernet cord to connect your computer directly to the router or modem.

* **A comfortable, well lit room.** Lighting is an important factor in virtual lessons. For the best effect, you want to avoid backlighting and try to have some light directly on your face. I

actually take a desk light and shine it right on my face when I do virtual lessons. It makes a huge difference.

❖ **A way to send money online.** Most teachers, including myself, require payment in advance of the virtual lesson. My virtual students usually pay me through PayPal, which requires a PayPal account. I'm also starting to use Square, which allows people to pay with credit and debit cards.

Nancy: How do I find a teacher who teaches virtual lessons?

Valerie: You can find most virtual teachers online, either by searching or going to YouTube. I've gotten most of my virtual students from my YouTube channel. Teachers who do virtual lessons will usually say so on their website or social media, but you can always email and ask!

Nancy: What happens next after you connect with a teacher?

Valerie: Once you and a teacher agree to work together, the first thing to do is find out what time zones you both live in. If you are both in the same time zone, it is much easier, but don't let that scare you from considering a teacher who lives further away! The first step is to share locations with your teacher and figure out the time difference. I use the World Clock Time Zone Converter.

Once you determine the time difference, you can find a time that works for both of you. If your chosen teacher is on the other side of the world, you may have to be creative to find a time. Also, be aware that not every country or even every state recognizes Daylight Savings Time changes, as in the US, so when those times come around, you need to re-address the lesson times accordingly.

Once you have your first lesson scheduled, you will need to either create an account on a platform like Zoom or Skype, or exchange phone numbers with FaceTime. Then after you take care of the payment, all you have to do is show up at your computer at your dedicated lesson time. You've done all the groundwork and prepared yourself for lessons with your new teacher, so now you can just relax in your own home and enjoy learning how to become a better singer. Enjoy the journey!

Nancy: Cool! Thanks Valerie! It's GREAT when you find out that you have a world of choices in finding a wonderful voice teacher. But, Oh No! How in the world do you find that wonderful teacher? Having Valerie as a teacher would be terrific (and you can contact her at vocalsplendor.com) but she can't teach everyone.

How Do I Find a Great Teacher?

This is an industry where anyone can say they are a voice teacher. There is no qualifying certification or master exam. So how do you know if a teacher is good for you?

Teachers You Don't Want To Study With

You might come across teachers who sell an overpriced method. "Pay $1,299 in 3 equal installments to have access to our <u>Ten Towers of Great Singing</u> ..." Or you might see younger teachers with cool videos and a loud voice pitching like a carnival barker about taking online lessons from them.

Sometimes experienced teachers can be a poor choice, too. Be wary of teachers who brag about themselves. For instance, I heard  a podcast by an established voice teacher who likes to talk about the people whose careers he has "launched." In this podcast, he said "When I discovered (the singing exercise) *Mesa di voce*, ...that felt like the miracle exercise to me." This might sound fine if you aren't paying attention to how he bends it to himself, but this is hundreds-year-old exercise used by millions and millions of singers. By saying "I discovered," he is making it about himself and elevating himself - as if he has unearthed the ultimate magic fix. It is subtle, but it is a common tactic throughout some teachers' marketing. If you interview a teacher and it seems like the conversation is more about how great the teacher is than what tools you need to develop, walk the other way. Likewise, if the teacher seems interested in how you can help his or her career, this is the wrong studio. It should be about you and how the teacher can help you reach your goals.

Not always, but oftentimes, new teachers can be a risky choice. Allen Henderson, Executive Director of the National Association of Teachers of Singing, said experienced teachers often tell one another, "I probably should contact all the students I taught my first five years and refund all the money they paid me." New teachers learn by what you teach *them.* If you want to study with someone who has been teaching for fewer than five years, only consider them if they have one or more of the following: a Master's Degree in voice, a mentor they actively work with, membership in the National Association of Teachers of Singing, or certification with a singing method program such as Somatic Voicework or Estill Voice.

Teachers You Do Want to Study With

I asked a room full of voice teachers what they thought was most important.

Here is the great list they came up with.
* Trust your instincts. If you like the teacher and trust the teacher, give them your trust.
* Feel you can become a team together - that the teacher is collaborating with you.
* Ask for referrals from other singers who you like to listen to: people who sing the way you would like to sing.
* Find a teacher who treats you respectfully, not abusively.
* Does your teacher give you full attention during the first lessons? Or does the teacher get distracted by a phone or email? Not ok.
* Find a teacher who communicates very clearly why you should do something - teaching you how to teach yourself, not leave you in the dark about why you are doing an exercise or assignment.
* The teacher should have an idea of curriculum - an idea of what your skill progression should be - to reach your goals

for the genre you have chosen or in multiple genres for a cross-training singer.

❖ The teacher needs to be open to developing you as a good performer, not just creating a good singer.

❖ You have to learn to give your trust to the teacher; trust that the teacher will help you transform over time. You will be on a long journey with that teacher. Don't expect overnight results.

There is so much noise that amazing teachers can have trouble being noticed. Prospective students can't tell who the best choice is for them. The students don't know if they are going to the real deal or the inexperienced person with glittery marketing. Often

times the amazing teacher, the one you really want, is so busy teaching that they don't do any marketing; they have a waiting list, and you should get on it!

If taking individual one-on-one lessons seems like the right direction for your path, there is no time like the present. In fact, the sooner you get started the better. Many of my students start at age 9 or 10, so by the time they get to college they have been studying for 8 years! Begin researching now and reach out to potential teachers. Ask for one or two first lessons (these are usually not free but are paid at the full rate) and then if it seems like a good fit commit to six months at a minimum. You will be amazed at how your singing improves.

Study Singing Through Choir

Singing in a choir or ensemble is a way to have fun while you work on your music reading, intonation skills, and other technical skills. A good choir can help you grow and strengthen your voice and learn how to interpret songs well. It can be at school, church, or in a community choir.

The teamwork of singing in a choir is a great thing. It is just as empowering as being on any team, but the best part is that you always win! Nobody can lose by being in a choir and it gives you a chance to build your voice and skills without putting your solo voice out there.

Singing in a choir is a lot more than just showing up, although one of the beauties of a choir is that if you aren't in the best shape,

vocally or emotionally, on any particular day, you can be on the quiet side and the choir will still be fine. But the best part of the choir is the teamwork - doing something that requires everyone to work together, in sync and without ego to mold the director's dream for a song.

When we stand in our section in a choir, we can't hear what the whole sound is like - we don't get to hear what the audience hears. Disappointing, right? But hang on; instead we get to be inside the machine. We get to hear and see how the individual parts work together.

We also learn a ton of singing skills in a choir. Good choir directors encourage students to improve their skills, their ears, and their vocal strength. For vocal strength, the more we sing, the better we get. It can't be helped. We are building the muscles when we sing and that makes our voices more accurate and improves the quality of our sound.

Just the act of matching our voices to the people around us requires us to listen and that improves our musical ear. We improve the way we hear when we spend time in a choir. And improving the way we hear others means we've also improved the way we hear ourselves - giving us a better ability to critique our own singing and increasing the likelihood we will stay in tune and in tempo.

Many directors also work with their singers to improve sight reading, ear training, and music theory skills. All three of these skills are essential to being a good singer. They may not make you sound better, but they make you into the kind of musician that other musicians want to work with. Nobody wants to work with a singer who doesn't talk or read the language. And learning the language is part of any skill we want to master. In a programming class, we learn to code in computer languages. In an art class, we learn the language for the techniques and tools. On a basketball team, we learn the language of the sport and how to read plays. And in choir, we learn the language of music and how to read it.

There is a warning, though. Voice teacher Kelly Stuible-Clark has this to say about her students in choir:

> I teach several students that are products of the high school choir - they meet every day for 50 minutes - and yes they're definitely a product of that instruction. Quality choir, fantastic musician leading them, but I have to explain to all of them that the sound Mr. D wants for Chorale is different than what we need for solo singing (especially musical theatre, which many of them come to me for). There may be some over exaggerated sounds, but I know he's asking for those tall overly rounded vowels that make a nice choral blend. Funny thing is, when I was in high school I wasn't one of the top singers because I could never modify my voice enough to sound like everyone else.

But being in a choir or ensemble isn't just about the skills. It's about the fun! Choirs get to express emotionally, share in the beautiful genius of the greatest composers of all time, and just have a blast goofing around together. Nothing is more fun than a choir trip!

Study Singing Through Shows

Singing in a show is a great way to have a ton of fun while mastering skills. There are lots of different kinds of shows: musicals, operas, operettas, musical revues, cabarets, madrigal dinners, and maybe you could even call a show choir a kind of show. In a show, singers need to cooperate intensely with their team, which includes the general director, the music director, the stage director, the instrumentalists, and the other performers. Together everyone works toward creating a great experience for the audience.

Singers in a show get to develop their solo voices more than singers in a choir but less than singers in voice lessons. There are also opportunities in almost every show to sing harmonies in small groups or the chorus. Doing both - solo singing and group singing - gives your brain the opportunity to develop lots of different skills. But it gets even better; in a show the singers need to perform while dancing, acting, and other movement. And almost all of it is going to be bigger than life and bring bigger than life fun.

But there is a price for building all of those skills. The price is *time*. It takes a lot of time to put together all the different parts and build all of the different skills (not to mention costumes, sets, and selling tickets). The actors in a high school or community show might work together for four months before finally performing for an audience. Some colleges, like the University of Houston, put on up to six operas a year! But not everyone is in every show. Summer theater (sometimes called Summer Stock) is a part time or full time summer job or camp where the actors learn the shows quickly and put them on for 3 months for tourists.

One of the biggest risks to a vocalist of being in a show is being encouraged to use a bad technique known as over-singing. Over-singing is when a singer puts too much effort (pushing air) into singing in the hope that it will make them louder. But this is a false idea and only leads to the singer sounding, looking, and feeling

strained. Singing isn't made louder by pushing more air. Imagine that your sound only went as far as your breath could carry it. It would fade away within 6 feet, and certainly never make it to the back of a theater. Instead, singing is made louder by resonance. A trained singer learns how to use resonance for loudness, and resonance modification helps singers create different styles of singing.

Another risk is singing while sick. Singing while sick means risking damage to the singer's vocal folds because "the show must go on."

Shows are a great way to make friends and have a really good time together. My favorite part of shows is the rehearsals, and saying goodbye after the last performance is always heartbreaking. To find a show to be in, look to your high school, community theater, opera company youth programs, or consider auditioning for summer stock theater.

Studying Professional Singers' Techniques

Most of the music we know deep inside of our hearts and souls is from professional recordings from our favorite singers, or songs we've heard over and over again on the radio. And that's great! We feel the emotions of the music, hear the amazing skills of the singers, and we bring them to life in our own voices when we sing along. Singing along is a great way to improve our own voices and skills. Sometimes the singers have amazing skills for great singing, sometimes great storytelling, and sometimes both.

You can learn so much from studying them - really noticing what they are doing and why. But think about this - the professional recordings are hardly ever one-take. They have always been altered - sort of like photoshopped - to sound perfect. Even professional video recordings released by the singer or a TV station have been altered to correct for pitch problems. And the cameras might break away from a singer to show an instrumentalist, so that we don't see if the singer cringes, coughs, signals to her back-up singers, or takes a drink of water. We never hear the unaltered voices of the singers unless we are listening to recordings from before 1980 (but even then engineers literally cut and pasted the tape to create the best version). A lot of times singers will admit that what they did in the recording studio - the amazing version we hear over and over - was just a fluke and they don't perform the song like that in public.

For example, Brandi Carlile had a big hit called "The Story." At the end of that song (just after 2:50) her voice shreds for just a few seconds. It sounds so raw and emotional - it is amazing! But the real story is that Brandi has only made that sound once, at 2 a.m. in the recording studio after an exhausting day when she was annoyed with her producer. The engineer and producer kept those few seconds and pasted them into the final version.

Another thing you'll hear is that on recordings singers belt (yell in an emotional, singing way) notes that, sometimes when they are performing live, they either sing legit (gentler voice) or don't sing at all. The performer may perform a song in a lower key than the recording because in the marathon of a concert, those original notes are too hard. So what can you believe? Listening to bootleg recordings from concerts (videos taken from the audience without permission) is a good way to hear those changes.

Your job is to study raw videos of performers in action.
- ❖ Watch the singers' faces and eyes for signs of what they are thinking about (also to notice who is lip syncing)
- ❖ Watch the singers' movements to see strategies for stamina

❖ Watch the singers' technique (especially posture, lips, and tongue) for how they deal with difficult parts
❖ Compare the raw version to the professional recording and notice changes. Question why they made changes.

Anyone absolutely anyone, can sound amazing in a professional recording. So don't set that artificial product as your measurement of success. Instead, try to be as good as your favorite singers are in live, raw performances. And learn everything they have to teach you - it is all there for you for free.

Mastering Emotional Expression

Mastering emotional Expression is a huge part of singing. Unlike a musician on any other instrument, singers' voices are affected by every physical and emotional reaction. Think of it this way, if you are talking to a friend on the phone, can you tell by their voice if they are happy, sad, grumpy, or bored? They usually don't have to tell you, you just know. But how do you know? It must be coming through in the sound waves. But how is that possible? Their voice, from leaving their mouth and entering the phone, has become digital signals on a data stream. What the heck? How could we know? Are we all psychics? That would be amazing, but probably not

Here's how we know. Deep inside of us we are programed to hear the little changes that muscle tension makes to our voices. We need to - it is survival. What we hear might be something obvious, like clipped-off, short words, or exaggerated consonants (those would be negative emotions). It might be a slow tempo and smooth phrasing (that would be calm). We can hear a smile, doubt, approval - no problem.

When singing, your audience expects to hear those things too. If a singer wipes all emotion from their interpretation, nobody is happy. But here is the problem, a singer might not feel like what their song is talking about. For instance, say you are in a great relationship but your song is about the jerk who broke your heart. You simply don't feel like that right now. In fact, maybe a jerk has never broken your heart and you don't know how that feels. That's where acting comes in.

Acting isn't a shallow layering on of a smile or frown, it is actually being happy or sad. The singer needs to find the emotions inside and express the emotion that the song is delivering. For some people, it comes very naturally. For others, it is really challenging. One of the reasons it might be challenging is that the emotions in the song are too strong, or too strange, to express and still sing. If you were to really feel that pain in a sad song, you would be a puddle on the floor. And if you really felt the excitement in a happy song, you'd be grinning so hard you couldn't sing! When that happens, it might be best to back away from the real

message of the song and imagine less of the emotion or a different but similar emotion.

For instance, imagine you are singing a song about an amazing tree that you greatly admire (bizarre, right? That is the plot of an awesome aria called *Ombra Mai Fu*). You might instead imagine that a lumber company is about to cut down a favorite old tree in your yard and you are pleading with them to not cut it down.

Here's another example: say you are singing a song about party girls who don't get hurt, or so they say, and push down their feelings. They feel like they might not make it to the morning. Singing that song could tie you up in knots if you really thought about the words - I can feel my gut tightening as I write about it - or it might be something that you can't relate to at all and you don't know how to act it. That's the plot of the song *Chandelier* by Sia. So what can you think about to express the right emotions? Well, that's on you to figure out. You need to interpret each sentence for what you want it to say - that is, what is the journey you are taking your listener on? The journey in your mind might be really different than the song lyrics. Like maybe you decide to imagine in your head, while singing *Chandelier*, about the day your sister beheaded your favorite doll, but you didn't tell on her because you didn't want her to tell on you about how you put your used gum under your bed. In that case the audience never needs to know the story in your head, as long as it makes your song interpretation just right.

For some people it is hard to "act" in front of family and friends because it feels like a lie. For them it is easier to perform a song with the right emotions when performing for strangers, or with a bright spotlight blinding the singer so they can't see the audience. Lots of times the best choice is to step into the character like a spirit inhabiting a character's body. Then it isn't really "you" performing the song, it is the character. I did that once when I was singing, *They Can't Take That Away From Me* by the Gershwin brothers. I have never experienced what the song is talking about, so the choice I made was to step into the body of a character who had experienced it.

Practicing mastering emotions in a song is something you can work on on your own, in a show, or in voice lessons. Having a teacher or mentor help you with acting is a great shortcut to figuring it out. There are independent acting teachers, just like there are independent voice teachers. The acting component of singing is super important, so don't forget to apply it to everything you perform.

Build Physical Skills

Warming up

What are warm-ups and which ones do I do?

Warmups help you wake up the muscles and improve flexibility. They are different from "vocal exercises" that teach you new skills.

Can everyone use the same warm-ups?
Yes, but maybe on different notes depending on how low or high the voice is.

Do I have to know how to play piano to do warm-ups?

No way! Since you are human, you have the very thing you need for the best kind of warm-ups - imagination. But if you are a lucky, modern human, you also have a computer and/or smart phone. Let's start with the imagination part and we'll get to the web part later. When I warm-up my favorite way, I use my imagination. Here's what I do:

First job: to warm up my high voice and my low voice.

Second: to warm up the big breathing muscles in the core of my body.

Third: to warm up the little muscles of my face and throat.

I also know I want to have fun doing it. And if you heard me warming-up, you would be completely positive that I am the worst musical theater villain you could ever imagine, like Cruella DeVil meets The Green Goblin from *Spider-Man: Turn Off the Dark*.

I usually start by howling like a wolf for 20ish seconds, then I moan like a zombie for another 20ish seconds. This gets the high and low parts going separately. Next I'll bring them together by taking a vocal roller coaster up, down, and all around for around a minute, making lots of different sounds.

If that wasn't villainous enough, my next task, to warm up the core muscles, is a good long, LOUD belly laugh followed by a nasty, nasal witches cackle. I do this for as long as it takes to feel literally warmer and more energized. It usually doesn't take long.

Final step is the face muscles. This can be silent - squishing up and then stretching your mouth, lips, and jaw muscles. But since I've already committed myself to the super villain, I go all out. I never know what sounds are going to come out - maybe machine guns, maybe a creaking door, a hissing snake, a raspberry. It's endless.

You can stop after a minute-ish. If you are warming up efficiently you only really need 3 - 5 minutes.

I will admit, I only do these kinds of warm-ups when I'm completely alone. In fact, I'm a little self-conscious just writing about it. If we meet and you look at me funny, I'll know why. But if you are feeling super brave, shoot a video of yourself doing your super villain warm-ups and share it with me on nancybos.net, Instagram, or Facebook.

There are ways to warm-up in much "nicer" methods with warmup songs and exercises randomly found on YouTube. It isn't nearly as fun and not quite as efficient. On the other hand, it isn't nearly as embarrassing.

The goals are basically the same - warm up high voice, low voice, core muscles, and face. They also have the added benefit of helping you train your ear (learning what to listen for).

Vocal Health

Vocal health is the most important information in this book. It's true that most of this book has been about following your passion and learning skills, but you can only achieve your goals if you have excellent, healthy vocal folds. Here are the basics you need to know for vocal health. If this is something that fascinates you, check out the website ncvs.org and the YouTube videos by Voice Body Connection contributor Elissa Weinzimmer.

What are Vocal Folds?

Vocal folds (also known as vocal cords) are in your neck, inside the hard cartilage cage of your voice box. There are two of them on either side of your windpipe. They act like a gate to the lungs, letting air go in and out of your lungs but snapping shut if food or liquid gets too close. The side benefit of vocal folds is that we can vibrate them against each other to make sound. In fact, that sound creation thing became such an important part of our evolution that we developed muscles around the vocal folds to really, really control what they can do, unlike a dog, pig, cat, or other animal which has a limited palette of vocal noises.

How To Take Care of Your Vocal Folds

We can't see our vocal folds unless we have a special camera or mirror like an Ear Nose and Throat (ENT) doctor has. It would be a lot easier to take care of our vocal folds if we could see them ourselves. But instead we use feeling and sound to tell us if we are treating our vocal folds well. The feeling that something is wrong

can be if it hurts to talk or if you feel like you have a lump in your throat. Alarm bells should be going off if you get hoarse easily, or your voice doesn't work well in the morning but gets better as the day goes on. If a person has what they think is a naturally raspy voice, it could mean that there is a lump or bump on the vocal folds that a doctor could help with. And if a person's voice feels really tired at the end of the day every day, it could be an issue for an ENT or a Speech Language Pathologist (SLP).

If we suspect there is something wrong, we go to the ENT to take a look. But it is also ok to start with a general practice doctor. They can tell you if there seems to be a good reason to see an ENT and can give you a referral.

But instead of thinking about when things go wrong, let's think about how to keep everything working just fine. For day-to-day vocal health for singers, there are some great tips to keep in mind:

1. Use the whole range of your voice every day. Stretch the muscles and ligaments by speaking and singing with high notes and low notes.

2. Wash your hands before touching your nose and mouth. Keep those germs away.

3. Get plenty of sleep. The more rested you are, the more likely you will use all the parts of your voice in their most efficient way.

4. Stay well hydrated. Vocal folds depend on moisture on their surface to work smoothly.

5. Don't smoke anything. Smoking is pulling polluted air into the lungs past the vocal folds. The vocal folds pick up a lot of the garbage carried in the smoke. It does short and long term damage.

6. If you are losing your voice, stop using your voice. If you are losing your voice from yelling, loud talking, or from being sick, stop using it until it has a chance to heal.

7. If the air is dry (dry climate, air conditioning, or forced-air heat) use a humidifier, especially at night.

8. Chill out when you can - stress can be the source of some vocal problems.

The big message I want you to take away from this chapter is to <u>be serious about your vocal health</u>. We each only get one set of vocal folds for our whole life. And there is only one person who notices how your vocal folds are doing every day - you.

You've got to be the protector of your vocal folds. Make sure that they aren't damaged by your other activities or lifestyle choices. And if you feel like something might already be wrong, talk to your doctor about it.

Build Musicianship Skills

If you've never taken voice lessons, or any music lessons, you might be stumped about how to even get started. It might seem like there are obstacles you could never get over, like not having a private place to practice, or not having the time or money for music books and lessons. And then there are the basic questions, like how do I know what to practice?

Well the good news is that just by picking up this book and reading the valuable information I'm giving you, you are taking some great first steps on your journey. We are going to talk about all of these obstacles. Plus, you'll find great support, materials, voice exercises, and advice at nancybos.net as well as some YouTube channels.

So let's get your life ready to add musicianship skills.

What resources do I need to be a better singer?
One of the first things you might be wondering is, **do I need to play piano or guitar to take singing lessons?** The answer is "*No-ish.*" But, learning how to play piano or guitar can only help. You see, it is really important for  singers to also become "musicians." That is, they need to learn

how to read sheet music, how to work in an ensemble like a choir or a group with instruments (like a band), and to learn what words like *arpeggio* and *rubato* mean. Some of that falls under the life-task of learning music theory. And a lot of music theory is taught by piano teachers. But there are other ways you can get music theory. If you aren't getting music theory some other way in your life, find an app or a book and add it to your homework. In my own voice studio, all of my beginning students study theory and ear training at every lesson, along with learning how to sing better and working on songs. So you see, I love it when singers are also musicians!

Another good reason to learn piano or guitar (or another instrument you can play while singing), is that instrumentalists who can sing have a competitive advantage when it comes to getting work over singers who don't play an instrument. The best thing is to be a singer *and* instrumentalist.

It used to be that a singer struggled to practice without a piano player to play their warm-up scales and the notes of their songs, and the cheapest way to have a piano player around was to learn to do it yourself. But now, thanks to online resources, we can get along just fine without a piano player until it comes to live performances. And even then, it has become acceptable to use a backing track in a lot of cases. So cross that off your list - you can begin without an instrument.

But there is one other thing you should know. If you plan to major in music in college, you will possibly need to pass a "Piano Proficiency Exam" by the end of your 2nd year. This exam can be tough, and I've known of plenty of people who had to change their academic direction because they couldn't play well enough to pass. In other colleges, there might not be a piano proficiency exam, but you might be required to accompany yourself on some instrument for a junior or senior recital.

Keyboard skills and guitar skills are
worth their weight in gold.

Another question might be, where do I practice?
Singing in front of family is one of the hardest things for a lot of people. We know we are going to sound bad sometimes, and we know we have to learn by making mistakes. We also know that anyone who is listening and cares about us is going to have an opinion, and that makes us uncomfortable. And being uncomfortable holds us back from really trying with exercises that might sound strange or silly. So stop right now and show this paragraph to whomever is helping you on this journey: your parents, your grandparents, your guardian - whoever it is. Show it

to anyone in the house. The thing they need to know is that you need a removed, private place to practice. And that they are not allowed to comment or judge on what they hear. Not even, "That exercise sounded great." The other people in the house need to ignore you, put on headphones, and go about their thing. When you are ready to show off, and do a little performance, you will let them know. In the meantime, you need to take a risk and do the sometimes ugly business of studying singing, without criticism.

Now this doesn't mean you need the entire living room to yourself. A bathroom, bedroom, or even closet will do just fine if you don't have your own bedroom. I used to take a music stand, pitch pipe, and (*ahem*) cassette player into the shower to practice. And if the weather was good, I'd sing in our garage.

The other thing your grown-up might be worried about is whether you will actually practice when you are alone or if instead you'll get distracted by things around you or the internet. That one is on you. You need to earn and deserve their trust. Prove to them that you will focus for 20 minutes each day and get the job done. You'll be a better singer for doing it, and they will be happier grown-ups.

Do I need sheet music?

The last item on the do-I-need-to-have list is sheet music. And again, nope! We are talking about imagination or the magic of the internet. Let's start with imagination. Do you remember when you were little and you used to make up songs? Did you sing to your toys, or did you sing about how much you hated your chores, or how sweet your pet was? Now think about your favorite singers. They sing songs that somebody made up, right? And we pay them to do that. It may seem like there is very little correlation between a pre-schooler singing to her doll and a star singing on stage. But actually, they have so much in common! All we need to do is make a bridge between them. At some point in life, most of us stopped making up songs. We let somebody else do it; we  let somebody else tell us what songs are good or right. But in our hearts, we still have a song.

So how do we build the bridge that will take us from little-kid songs to big-kid songs? One melody at a time. Go back to that little kid stage. Sing to your socks, your big toe, and your knee caps - left and right. Don't record it, in fact, barely even listen to yourself. Let your brain have fun passively learning while you goof around with singing. There is a good chance that over time - and I'm talking months and years - those songs will become more coherent (when you want them to be), and you might even find that some want to be written down. The key thing is now while your brain is growing and nobody is forcing you to pump out "good" songs, is to enjoy the gift you were given in early childhood. Turn life into your own grand musical.

I love living in the "personal musical" idea - it is one of my favorite places to be. But we have to face it, there are some great songs out there and we ought to sing them. In fact, we get to sing them. Genius music writers are putting songs out there every day and it is great to share in their amazing work. There are lots of ways to find and sing this music: karaoke files with lyrics on YouTube, backing tracks on Spotify and iTunes, singing apps like Wurrly, and sheet music sites like sheetmusicdirect.com and onlinesheetmusic.com.

You might have noticed that in this whole chapter about musicianship, most of it sounds like a lot of fun. The only thing I'm asking you to do that isn't singing is to learn music theory and sight reading. So what is music theory?

Music theory can be broken down into three big categories:

1. The language and structure of music so that we can communicate musical concepts to others and follow commonly used formulas for note relationships.
2. The history and sources of music in different parts of the world.
3. The basic structural differences between different styles of music.

Let me try that again. Here are those same three points in a little different wording.

Being a good musician means:

1. You can talk about music in a way that other musicians understand what you mean.
2. You've got a pretty good grip on the sources of current styles - like where did jazz come from and where did opera come from?
3. When you compare different styles of music you can tell what they are and why: blues vs. classical vs. Bollywood vs. musicals.

These are the basic foundations of musicianship: theory, practice, discipline, and creativity. Finding a way to do and enjoy all four will go a long way to making you a well-rounded musician.

Time Practicing vs. Time Performing

> *I have yet to hear these words uttered in my studio:*
> *"I have too much time on my hands.*
> *I need more to practice."*
> *Students are often overwhelmed at the number of things that they are being asked to do. When they have free time they usually want to play or sleep.*
>
> From *Six Word Lessons for Exceptional Music* Lessons by Sally Palmer

In the previous chapter, you might have noticed that I said, "focus for 20 minutes each day and get the job done." You might be asking, "Really? Only 20 minutes?" or you might be asking, "Holy cow, where am I going to find 20 minutes every day?" And guess what, depending on which question you are asking tells a lot about singing for you. If 20 minutes of practice sounds like too little, GREAT! And if 20 minutes sounds like too much for your busy life, you'll need to make more room in your life for it if singing is a high priority for you.

Twenty minutes per day is the minimum. Just like working out your body, we need to work out our voices every day. If we sing deliberately for 20 minutes every day (including choir and show rehearsals), we will see the benefits of sounding better, being able to sing longer, and learning the music as well as new skills. If we don't practice deliberately for 20 minutes every day, we will not sound better, will not increase how long we can sing, will not learn the music, and will not increase our skills. It's that simple.

But can you sing for more than 20 minutes each day? You bet! You can sing until your voice starts to get tired enough that it doesn't feel good to sing, or until you start to notice that your tone is getting fuzzy or a little hoarse. Then stop for the day and don't sing again until tomorrow.

There will be times when you have a lot of performance demands. Especially if you are in a show or your choir has a series of concerts. At those times you'll want to back off from practicing. You might find that your voice gets tired from the other activities and that you need a break until your schedule gets back to normal.

How does this compare to instrumentalists who might practice for 3 or more hours every day? The big difference is that for all those other instruments, the actual sound making is outside of the body and not made of soft tissue. Our vocal folds are not as resilient as a violin string or the reed on a saxophone. They aren't made out of wood or metal. And we can't replace them - ever. So if you find you want to spend more time working on singing but not so much actual singing, use your time to study your music, analyze other singers performance videos, research new music, and read articles and blogs about singing. All of those things count as practice time.

Performance Anxiety

I'm going to tell you a story about my Grandma. Her name was Esther and she she was a tall, strong farmer with a large presence. She lived with my Grandpa Harold. They grew corn outside of a small town in Iowa. By small, I mean minuscule. Population 840. There were two churches in this town: Catholic and Lutheran. They went to the Lutheran church - early service - at 8:30 every Sunday morning. They sat six rows from the front on the left side. The church was usually pretty full; the right side was full all the way, front to back. The left side was full for the back half. But the first five rows on the left usually had only a few people in them - often guests. You see, Grandma Esther was a terrible singer. Her voice was harsh, kinda yelly, and her pitches were usually near the mark but not quite on. But Esther sang out and she sang loud. She loved the old Lutheran hymns and wanted nothing more than to praise her God in song. So now you know why there weren't a whole lot of people sitting front left - sitting in front of Esther was very challenging.

But her passion for singing from her heart out to God was undeniable. And no one in that church told her to hold back or stop. They all understood her need to sing out. Chances are that you are more self-conscious about your singing than Grandma Esther was. Most everyone is. And that means you are holding your voice back in some way so that you don't offend or annoy others, or embarrass yourself. Where in your life are you experiencing less joy in singing than you should? Is there a time that you are expressing yourself less authentically than you could be when it comes to singing?

Every human has descended from singers. Singing is core to being human. Every culture on every continent has a singing tradition. We can express so much more through singing than with speaking alone - that's why music is so great! Even cartoons like Stephen Universe and The Simpsons use songs when the characters want to express something really deep - deeply evil, sincere, or silly. Singing is a basic human need. And you should have the confidence to express yourself through song just like anyone else. If you don't have that confidence, then let's get started on building it.

Stopped in Your Tracks - Solving the Performance Anxiety Problem

When it comes to people who deserve to have over-the-top confidence, Taylor Swift could be near the top of that list. Taylor started crafting songs and performing at age 5. She released her first album at 16. She came from a family of musicians; her grandmother was an opera singer! Taylor worked at her musicianship and performing skills for so much of her childhood that she got to sing *The Star-Spangled Banner* at a Philadelphia

76ers game at the age of 11! When Taylor was 16 she released her first single, *Tim McGraw*, and the song became a Top 10 hit on the country charts! It also appeared on her debut album that same year, which sold more than 2.5 million copies!

That should be enough to make a person confident, right? If that wasn't proof that she was good enough and people loved her, what could be? In 2008 she released an album called Fearless - even more evidence that Taylor shouldn't have nerves! But there's more. She was ranked No. 1 as the highest paid celebrity under 30 in 2012, beating out Justin Bieber, Rihanna and Lady Gaga, with a salary of $57 million!

So it might be a massive surprise that in a 2012 interview with MTV, Taylor said, "I get nervous -- really, really, really nervous. There's a point where you feel like, 'OK, this is pretty close to cruise control; we're on the stage, I'm walking, my legs are working right, it's fine. You're not shaking, you're great, everything's cool.'

You can get yourself there mentally, but I definitely get nervous before I go on."

Does it make any sense that Taylor Swift was still nervous after all that success and love from the world? No Way! It makes no sense at all. But she's not alone. Beyoncé, one of the most iconic singers of this century, said "I get nervous when I don't get nervous. If I'm nervous, I know I'm going to have a good show."

What does it mean when these amazing and successful women get nervous about performing? Does it mean that the rest of us should shut down and give up? Nope! It means just the opposite. We have to deal with the nerves and not let them stop us. Nerves may not mean what you think they mean; that you are not ready or that you are not good enough. And that feeling nervous is normal.

Lots of thought and research has been given to performance anxiety over the years. Brilliant people have poured hours of work into why humans get nervous and how to overcome it. All that work has filtered down to some pretty clear instructions. And luckily, we can learn those strategies, apply them to ourselves, and take the amazing journey beyond the nerves that stop so many people.

Nervousness, and singers' thoughts about nervousness, have changed entire careers and lives, and not for the better.

Thousands and thousands of people have avoided sharing their musical gifts because of nerves. Performers have shaken, sweated, and even cried on stage, and vowed to never sing in front of an audience again. Singing in front of an audience can be one of the most emotionally challenging things in life. No wonder we run away from it! Just the thought of it sort-of makes me want to stop this book right here! Just talking about being nervous with you has made my heart beat faster, my breath a little shallower, and I noticed I'm a little warm. Performance anxiety seems not-real or made-up, all in your head. Much of it IS in your head, but it sure does have real physical effects

To help us grow past our performance nerves, I've brought in expert Peak Performance Music Coach Diana Allan. Diana wrote

the book on confidence on stage for singers. She gives presentations all over the world on peak mental conditions for performers. And we are so lucky to be able to take her great advice and apply it to our own singing!

Nancy: Diana, it seems like some people get really, really nervous on stage, and other people have no problem. What can a girl do if nervousness is holding her back?

Diana: How right you are Nancy! Lots of singers, young and old, inexperienced and experienced get nervous--really nervous. What most of them have concluded is that their nerves mean that something is WRONG. This WILL hold a girl back and could not be further from the truth. A singer's nervousness indicates that she cares a great deal about her music. I bet the girls reading this book agree. They really love to sing and want to sing their best. What can be wrong with this? This desire can make them worry about being good enough. It may even cause them to worry that they could embarrass themselves or disappoint themselves, their parents, or teachers by making mistakes, forgetting words, or messing up. This fear of embarrassment or  disappointment can trigger the primitive reptilian brain that is still in each of us.

Nancy: Reptilian brain?

Diana: Yes, it is the source of your oldest and most powerful coping mechanism--the fight-flight-freeze response--that revs your body up to protect itself. Just think of your great, great, great, great caveman grandmother. A rival tribesman or a charging lion were threats or dangers that triggered her fight-flight-freeze response. Our brains are wired to protect ourselves--even if what you are needing to protect is your reputation or other people's opinions of you.

Nancy: So being nervous to sing is a little bit related to being actually scared for your life? I know you have a lot to teach us, Diana, so how about you take the rest of this chapter.

Diana: Sure, I'd love to give a whole lot of information and ideas to help singers have more fun and have fewer of the kind of nerves that get in the way of performing. When *you* perceive a threat (making a mistake) or danger (embarrassing yourself), *you* react, too!

These reactions can fall into one of the following categories:

> *Physical: shaking, heart racing, sweating, upset stomach, headache*
> *Mental: repetitive negative thoughts (worry, fear, doubt), difficulty concentrating*
> *Emotional: unhappiness, fearfulness, helplessness, confusion*

Once you get into the habit of thinking of singing or performing as being threatening or dangerous, it can be difficult to stop, but over time you can learn better ways to react.

Palms sweaty? Heart racing? Stomach in knots? Cotton mouth?

Life in danger? Being chased by a monster?

Nope, just getting ready to sing my solo!

Take Courage: Trust and Accept

Accepting that it may be ok to be nervous and that most people are, will help you realize that good performers often find it necessary to have a certain amount of nervousness in order to perform their best. You might want to think of it this way. There is a fine line between nervousness and excitement. I was struck by this very fact a few years ago when I was coaching a young singer who was so keyed up and nervous, she would be queasy and could not sleep the night before important performances. It triggered a memory for me of having that same trouble every Christmas Eve. I would lie in bed tossing and turning and unable to sleep. I was so keyed up by the anticipation of the following day--my stomach upset, my heart racing, and my mind awhirl. This is exactly what the young singer described with one VERY important exception--our perceptions of these thoughts and feelings. One of us interpreted these thoughts and feelings as nervousness and the other as excitement. So which is it--nervousness or excitement. Believe it or not, that is really up to you! It's all about your point of view. It is just as easy to conclude that you are excited as it is to conclude that you are nervous. Either way, you will want to learn to embrace the butterflies you feel and train them to fly in formation to work for you.

Pressure makes coal, but it also makes **diamonds!**

Trust

Singers who are good butterfly trainers are those who are able to shush their inner critic and focus on what is most important to performing their best. The bottom line is they **trust** themselves and their practice. These performers define **trust** as

| *the ability to let go of conscious control over being correct.*

Trust is also the *absence* of unrealistic expectations (like trying to be perfect or pleasing everyone all of the time) and the *absence* of judgments (like thinking you know what others are thinking or know you will mess up). Trust is not only a primary performance skill, it is a performer's ultimate goal!

Why is it difficult for some singers to trust themselves and their abilities?

What a good question! It may surprise you to realize that musicians spend the majority of their time practicing and preparing to perform rather than actually performing. Whether a beginner or a professional, that makes us practicers, not performers! Because we are more used to practicing (working technically, analyzing, evaluating), it is easy to get stuck in the practice mode and can be difficult to shift to the performance mode.

What are these two modes and which one is better?

There are two modes or mindsets that singers--or any musician--needs: the practice mindset and the performance mindset. Both are equally important. The practice mindset is a set of specific skills that are necessary to improve and refine technical or performing ability:

Practice Mindset
- ❖ Conscious control (acquiring skill)
- ❖ Questioning
- ❖ Evaluating
- ❖ Trying hard
- ❖ Impatience
- ❖ Working for future improvement

These skills fall into one of three categories:
- ❖ Ability to self-monitor for correctness
- ❖ Ability to self-instruct
- ❖ Ability to analyze for cause and effect after mistakes

These skills are great for practice, but when you take them onto the stage with you = *Anxiety*!!!

The problem is: many singers get *stuck* in the practice mindset and don't turn these skills off when it's time to perform. Anxiety likes nothing better than when you're stuck in the practice mindset. When you perform, you need to *shift* into the performance mindset.

Performance Mindset

❖ Subconscious or automatic control (reliance on skill already acquired)
❖ In-the-moment thinking
❖ Accepting
❖ Allowing
❖ Patience
❖ Performing for now

The performance mindset is very different from the practice mindset. In the performance mindset, you need to easily:

❖ Maintain a clear and present *focus* and
❖ Trust yourself and your preparation.

Singers need *both* mindsets in order to develop *trust*. Practicing for *trust* means shutting off the practice mindset and switching to the performance mindset. Getting *stuck* in the practice mode is one of the primary sources of anxiety. You need both mindsets to become a successful performer.

Learning to trust yourself and your abilities sets the stage for *acceptance* -- the non-judgmental mindset of performance; performance mindset. When you accept yourself and your current abilities, you are free to perform without judgments as to right or wrong and good or bad. What a relief!

Constantly judging your performances can bleed over into your non-performing life. When you can't let a mistake go, it can be a *sure sign* that you are equating your performing with your personal worth. Let me illustrate this point with a story:

What if I were to come up to you on the street and offer you a $20 bill? You would probably take it, right? You reach out for it and I say, "I'm going to give this $20 bill to you, but first I need to crumple it into a little ball." You look at me like I'm crazy, but you reach out for it. I hold out the horribly wrinkled bill and ask, "You don't want it like this, do you? You nod and reply, "Yes, I do." I am surprised by your answer and quickly, to your horror, toss the bill on the ground and stomp on it. After I pick it up and dust it off, I hand it to you again, "Do you still want it now?" I am assuming you would nod again and take the $20. Why not?

This story teaches a valuable lesson about your life as a performer. No matter what I did to the money, you still wanted it. Why? Because its value never changed. Even though it was crumpled and dirty, it was still worth $20. Sometimes you may feel crumpled and ground into the dirt by the decisions you make or the circumstances that come your way. The next time you feel that you are not good enough, remember this story and that no matter what happens to you--no matter how well or how poorly you think you performed, whether you made a mistake, forgot your words, think you disappointed someone or embarrassed yourself--your worth will NEVER change. Your worth comes not from what you *do*, or who you know or impress, but from *who you are*. You have *infinite* worth -- no matter what!

Learn to Use It

> "I can never be safe; I always try and go against the grain. As soon as I accomplish one thing, I just set a higher goal. That's how I've gotten to where I am." – Beyoncé Knowles

How can singers build their trust and acceptance?
Building trust and acceptance takes courage. For those of us who get nervous, we are either already stuck in the practice mindset, really used to being fearful, or experts at judging ourselves. It takes courage to break the bonds of these habits and build new

and better ones, but it can be done. There are several effective strategies that, if practiced like your other musical skills, can help you learn to courageously accept and trust yourself and your abilities. When you accept and trust yourself more, you will have more fun and you will have fewer of the kind of nerves that get in the way of your performing (fewer/smaller butterflies to train!).

Let's take a look at the primary strategies I teach performers:

- ❖ Create more performance opportunities for yourself (practicers vs performers)
- ❖ 80-20 Practice Plan
- ❖ Declare Your Practice Complete
- ❖ Confidence Résumé
- ❖ Simulate Performance
- ❖ Adversity Practice

More Performance Opportunities

If your nervousness interferes with your performing, the first strategy you need is to create more performing opportunities for yourself. You need PRACTICE handling your nerves and trusting and relying on your preparation. Contact a local library, talk to friends, and see if a local coffee shop might like some free live music. At the holidays get a bunch of friends together to put on a holiday show for your parents. Perform more!

80-20 Practice Plan

Performers can also practice ACCEPTANCE and TRUST by using the two-step 80-20 Practice Plan:

Step 1 of this plan, when learning new music or practicing a new skill, is to spend at least 80% of each practice session in the Practice Mindset; acquiring/refining new skills. The other 20% of the practice session, if even a short phrase or two, is **performing**. This is the part of your practice session when you will practice shifting to the performance mindset. Remember that you need to include performing (practice turning off your evaluating thoughts) in **EVERY** practice session.

PRACTICE for CORRECTNESS	PERFORM
80%	20%

As a performance nears, flip the equation to 20-80: taper off practicing for correctness to 20% in favor of practicing TRUST for 80%. This strategy will go a long way towards enabling you to practice Trust and Acceptance

PERFORM, TRUSTING PREPARATION	PRACTICE
80%	20%

Declare Your Practice Complete

Declaring your practice complete is closely associated with the 80-20 Plan except on steroids! and can help us learn a special lesson. In master classes she teaches, Broadway star Sierra Boggess (Ariel in <u>The Little Mermaid</u> and Christine in <u>The Phantom of the Opera</u>), passes along a quote from one of her first teachers: "You are enough, you are so enough, it's unbelievable how enough you are." This is so true, but so many singers fail to

recognize it. Declaring your practice complete involves accepting that for today, *you are enough*. The way this strategy works is that a couple of days before a performance you "Declare your Practice Complete!" That's right! You *quit* practicing to make the piece better. You *only* practice *performing*!! This helps you (actually forces you) to shift into the performance mindset. If you are singing a whole set or a whole recital, you may want to declare your practice complete for up to 5 days prior to the performance. This strategy gives you ample opportunity to *accept* yourself for being truly *enough* for this performance! It takes courage to do this, but thinking, "I want to share where I am today with this piece" is much better than being stuck in the practice mindset and living with the anxiety that produces.

Confidence Résumé

When thinking about being enough, you might need some reminders that you actually *are*! This is where the Confidence Résumé comes in. Confidence is the *strength* of your belief in yourself and your abilities. Sometimes we need reminding! At some point in your life, you will construct a performance résumé that documents for others all of your education and accomplishments. When you go to auditions, you will present your résumé to directors. A **confidence résumé** will differ from your performance résumé in one  very important way--its use. Your performance résumé is for others to learn about you and assess your experience. Your confidence résumé is for you to affirm yourself and reinforce your own strengths.

What's on a confidence résumé? Your résumé will be a list of "I statements" that can answer the following questions:

* ❖ What are the strongest parts of your **performing** or **singing**? (I'm very expressive.)

- How would you describe your skills to others if they wouldn't think you were bragging? (I have a beautiful voice, I'm a great sight reader.)
- What can you say about your training that gives you confidence? (I've got a great teacher who really helps me sing my best.)
- What can you say about your **commitment** to or **work ethic** in music? (I work really hard!)
- How are others supportive of your music that helps you feel confident? (I've been selected as first chair or as soloist many times.)
- What have you accomplished in your performing that makes you most proud? (I won ..., I was selected...)
- What have others complimented you on in your performing? (Others say that I am good at connecting with the audience when I am performaning.)

Just the act of constructing your confidence résumé can boost your confidence and can get your eye off of what's missing in your performances and on what you already possess for success. The next step is to keep it updated. Add successes and accomplishments as they occur. Print it out, post it in your locker or on your bathroom mirror, and refer to it often. Taking your confidence résumé backstage with you and referring to it just prior to going on the stage is a good way to keep your mind on what will help your performance.

Simulate Performance

Simulating performance conditions is important to practicing how you are going to handle nerves and use them to help you perform your best. Whenever possible, try to "practice" in the actual space you will perform. The simulate performance strategy is all about trying to recreate in practice the conditions you will face in performance. If this is not possible, simulate the space--create spotlights by taking the lampshades of the lamps in your room (ask your parents, ok?), try to find a room that might have similar acoustics, wear the clothes and shoes you intend to perform in, and ask friends or peers (who make you nervous) to come in to listen. When simulating, you want to re-create the TOTAL experience as closely as possible. This includes preparing for distractions.

Adversity Practice

Adversity Practice can increase your trust and acceptance because it sharpens and narrows your focus and concentration. It helps you "practice" focusing on what is most important during performance. Not all distractions are created equal. First, *make a list* of things that distract you the most and then *simulate* these in your practice.

_____

_____

_____

_____

The following is a list of distractions and suggestions for this type of practice:

DISTRACTION/ADVERSITY	PRACTICE STRATEGY
elevated heart rate or out of breath	sing after quickly climbing 2 flights of stairs or jumping rope
forget words	sing while someone is talking in your ear
getting cold	sing with windows open (in winter) or fan on
getting over-heated	sing while wearing a heavy coat
audience movement	sing while having friends/family try to distract you

It is important for you to remember that it is NORMAL to be a little anxious or to feel butterflies before a performance. If your nervousness doesn't go away once you start singing or you are *so* nervous that it is hard to sing your best when it really matters, then it's time you pay attention to your mental as well as your musical preparation. When you do, you can learn effective strategies you need to help you use your nervousness to your advantage! Some performers find it helpful to reach out to a performance coach. A performance coach can help you identify what your unique strengths and challenges and guide you on your journey.

Thank you so much Diana!

You can learn more from Diana about mastering the performance mental game on the Peak Performance for Musicians website www.musicpeakperformance.com

What do you do from here? Read this section from Diana Allan over and over. Use a highlighter on the parts you want to remember and apply. And start writing your Confidence Résumé!

Sample Confidence Resume

What are the strongest parts of my performing or singing?

_____

_____

_____

_____

_____

What skills could I brag about if I wanted to?

_____

_____

_____

_____

_____

What about my training gives me confidence?

_____

_____

_____

_____

How is my commitment or work ethic in music?

_____

_____

_____

_____

How do other people treat me regarding music that helps me feel confident?

_____

_____

_____

_____

_____

_____

What are my performance accomplishments that make me proud?

_____

_____

_____

_____

_____

What have others complimented me about in my performing?

_____

_____

_____

_____

_____

_____

PART 3: PICKING YOUR PATH

We made it. We've decided what state you are heading toward; remember that problem of traveling from Texas and ending up anywhere from Charlotte, NC to Montreal, Quebec without a map? In Part 1 we started to build a map of your goals based on what is in your heart and what is also smart. In Part 2 we explored the skills you'll need to build to get there. Now it is time to get specific; it is time to make some really big decisions.

Here's another look at the "three basic, really big, well-traveled paths to a life in singing" we talked about at the end of Part 1.

Goal #1
I want to be a successful, full-time professional singer.

Path #1
Now might be the time to sing, perform, network, master an instrument, and post high quality

videos and audio that you won't regret later. Once your regular fan base grows, build your mailing/subscriber list. Go to summer performance camps and go to workshops all year. Work hard on your DIY career and start now.

Goal #2
I want to be a serious well-rounded musician.

Path #2
Study deliberately and with focus. Perform some. Build skills and network. Learn all you can.

Goal #3
I love to sing but it's not everything.

Path #3
Sing for your own enjoyment and the enjoyment of your community. Consider also gaining skills in complementary interests, like business, audio engineering, video production, voice science, costume design, music therapy, and music

Sing for your own enjoyment and the enjoyment of your community. Consider also gaining skills in complementary interests, like business, audio engineering, video production, voice science, costume design, music therapy, and music ministry.

♦♦♦

Our next step is to look at potential careers based on *heart* and *smart*.

There are many, many singing related careers to choose from. This list includes jobs that are *not* a professional singer. But it also includes careers that are for professional singers but not soloists. And for that rare solo career, we'll cover that in depth in the next chapter. Go through this section with a pencil or a highlighter. Cross out the ones that sound terrible and highlight the ones that are really interesting. Those interesting ones are the careers you want to learn more about.

◆◆◆

Arts Management (aka Arts Administration)

These are the leaders of arts organizations like theater companies and opera houses. The ideal Arts Manager will have business acumen and a deep understanding of the art their organization delivers to the public. Many Universities offer master's degree programs in Arts Management.

www.internationalartsmanager.com

www.artsmanagement.net

Speech-Language Pathologist (aka Speech Therapists)

While these clinicians are known for helping patients with stutters and lisps, the job involves a large variety of issues involving the body's ability to communicate using the voice. This can cover anything from trouble swallowing to vocal nodes in singers. In the U.S., this job requires a master's degree in Communicative Disorders/Speech-Language Pathology, and

doctoral programs are available. Those who specialize in treatment of vocalists are sometimes called "Voice Therapists."
www.asha.org/Students/Speech-Language-Pathology
voicefoundation.org

Vocologist
This is a relatively new field which specializes in rehabilitating and/or strengthening voices with a deep understanding of science. The Vocologist is a voice teacher with additional certifications, or a speech pathologist with performance training, who assists a medical team. There are university vocology programs available in the U.S., India, and Italy.
www.pava-vocology.org
www.ncvs.org

Music Therapist
Music Therapy is a proven technique used in Neuropathy to treat physical and mental issues. Music Therapists work in a wide variety of specialties such as memory work with the elderly, developmental assistance for patients with special needs, and physical therapy rehabilitation. You might find this job at hospitals, schools, or even correctional facilities. Degrees in Music Therapy are available on all academic levels.
www.musictherapy.org

Primary/Secondary School Music Teacher

This is a job most High School students will be very familiar with! Specialization options include not just instrument(s)/voice and music theory but also many unique methodologies such as the Suzuki method and the Kodály Method. It is worth noting that there are often strict degree/certification requirements for teaching in public schools; these vary by location. (There are also pre-school positions available with organizations like Kindermusik.)

nafme.org

www.mtna.org

Post-Secondary School Music Teacher (Professor)

Most of these college-level educators specialize in vocal (or instrumental) performance, music theory, music history, or composition. Typically, universities require a doctoral degree for this position.

nafme.org

www.mtna.org

Diction and Speech Coach

Voice and Speech professionals work with lots of different people for how they speak, like actors, professional speakers, and voiceover people. They can also help opera singers on proper articulation of the words in the libretto. The diction coach may also facilitate pre-performance vocal warm-ups and teach proper technique for reducing vocal damage.

www.vasta.org

Opera Director

This is a specialization option for a Stage Director which requires knowledge of opera rehearsal processes, and a knowledge of and love for opera as an art form. A director is responsible for coordinating the collaboration of all creative staff in a stage production. Most stage directors have at least a bachelor's degree in theatre production or a related field.

sdcweb.org

Professional Choral Singer

There are professional choirs all over the world, and especially in Los Angeles for film and TV, which pay their members the same way a symphony orchestra pays its musicians. However, most professional choristers work for religious organizations to lead worship music. This is not a job which usually pays all the bills on its own, but can be done in conjunction with other work (like teaching or studio musicianship), and it can be a rewarding one.

www.choirplace.com

Songwriter

This is a field with a lot of different niches. Your success writing words and music for other performers is largely measured by how popular those performances become. Songwriters also must have some performance skill themselves for creating demo recordings for musicians and music publishers. A successful songwriter also exhibits persistence and strong business skills. There are degrees available in this field, but advanced study is not required.

www.songwritersguild.com
www.ascap.com/songwriter

americansongwriter.com

Music Supervisor (aka Music Director)
The Guild of Music Supervisors defines music supervisor as "A qualified professional who oversees all music related aspects of film, television, advertising, video games and any other existing or emerging visual media platforms as required." A broad understanding of music is essential to this role, as are strong business networking skills and legal knowledge. There is no set educational path.

www.guildofmusicsupervisors.com

www.songwriteruniverse.com/music-supervisors-directory.htm

Audio Engineer (aka Recording Engineer, Sound Engineer)
These highly-skilled technicians use recording equipment to shape the sound of a recorded performance. Sometimes, this person also fills the role of Music Producer. Formal education is not required for this job, but degrees in the field are offered at many universities.

www.aes.org

Music Producer
The producer oversees all aspects of creating recorded music. This includes writing and arrangement, and technical engineering. Sometimes, this person also fills the role of Audio Engineer. This job requires advanced and up-to-date technical knowledge, as well as very good business management and networking skills.

www.ampnow.com

pmamusic.com

Voice Teacher

A voice teacher helps students to develop their singing skills, including technical sound production and performance. Some are on staff at universities, while others run their own independent studio. A variety of formal degrees will prepare you be a voice teacher, especially those focusing in vocal pedagogy.

www.nats.org

Choral Director

The director of a choir conducts rehearsals, recruits singers, selects music, and leads/organizes performances. A choral director may work for a church, school, or orchestra, or in rare cases, they may direct an independent performing group. Many universities offer bachelor's and advanced degrees in choral direction.

acda.org

www.choraldirectormag.com

Otolaryngologist

Also known as a specialized Ear, Nose and Throat (ENT) doctor, these physicians diagnose and treat diseases in these areas, and other structures of the neck and face. This position requires fifteen years of formal training and (in the US) a certification from the American Board of Otolaryngology, plus additional training for any specializations.

www.aboto.org

Director of Music Ministry

This person organizes all worship music for a religious organization. Depending on the size of the organization, this could mean anything from directing a small choir of volunteers to managing a team of music professionals. There are some formal degree programs available in this field, but most Music Ministry Directors enter the field first as a choir director or accompanist.

www.nacmhq.com

www.worshipmusician.com

Teaching Artist (aka Artist Educator)

A Teaching Artist is a professional artist who teaches with the perspective of a working performer. They can be employed by arts organizations such as opera companies and symphonies, or schools and community organizations. No formal education is required, but skills in teaching and experience as a working artist are essential.

www.teachingartists.com/whatisaTeachingArtists.htm

teachingartistsguild.org

Voice Actor

These professionals find work in any setting where a character can be heard without the actor being seen. These mediums included animated film, dubbed foreign entertainment, radio, audiobooks, video games, and documentaries. No formal training is required, but acting (and sometimes singing) skills are a must-have. Business networking skills will also be useful to these professionals.

www.world-voices.org

Cantor

A cantor is a solo singer who leads traditional religious music. In the Jewish tradition, they are called Hazzanim and are recognized as clergy. There are formal education options for Catholic and Jewish cantorial training. This title can also refer to a "precentor" or "protopsaltis" in the Christian tradition where precise duties will vary by organization.

www.cantors.org

Session Singer (aka Studio Musician, Backing Vocalist)

These performers provide temporary back-up for solo performers in recording sessions. They may also work for recording studios on advertising or soundtrack recordings. They rarely become well-known, but can gain wide respect within the music industry. Required skills include musical versatility and professional reliability. Also helpful are the abilities to harmonize and sight-read. A formal music degree is an option, but not necessary.

www.sagaftra.org

Music Arranger

An arranger transforms a melody into a full-fledged musical piece for performance. This requires advanced knowledge of music theory, and business networking skills. No formal degree is required, but many are offered.

www.asmac.org

Stage Manager

This person oversees the technical aspects of a live performance, including lighting and sound tech. They support the director, actors, and designers, and supervise the stage crew. Business management skills are a must, as well as extensive experience with stage productions. Formal training is not required, but is offered at many universities.

www.stagemanagers.org

This was a sample of some careers you can consider in order to have a balanced and fulfilling life full of singing. There are many more possible careers.

(Special thanks to Meghan Moore for filling out this list for us, and to CareersinMusic.com for being an excellent resource.)

Career As A Professional Singer

This highly competitive field can lead to fulfilling part-time work, a full-time career, or (rarely) fame and fortune. In addition to musical talent, training, and experience, a successful performer will have sharp business acumen. The ability to find work depends on your networking skills. Performers of every level will be applying for jobs (auditioning) almost constantly. This job does not require any degree, but many are offered.

www.actorsequity.org/

www.afm.org/

www.grammy.com/recording-academy

But first, before you decide that you want to be a professional singer, decide what kind of singing.

What Style Should I Sing?

It might seem like an easy answer - you have no doubt what style to sing. Or maybe it is exactly the opposite - you have no idea what to sing. Either way, I have some ideas to help you pick the best path for you. I'll break it down into three scenarios: I've Got This, Any and All, and Style?

I've Got This

You've probably grown up with a favorite kind of music. Maybe it's all R&B or country, or maybe you are totally driven by musical theater. Sometimes a person's favorite kind of music is the music of their community, like Bluegrass, Klezmer, or Contemporary Christian. There's even a chance that you are passionate about Barbershop or Opera. And I love that! It is great to know what kind of music you are passionate about and become an expert in that music. Becoming an expert in the style you want to sing gives you a huge advantage in lessons.

However, there's a downside. The downside is if there isn't someone to mentor you on that path - if there isn't a teacher to teach you what you need to know. So now you need a plan. You need a way to get great at the style of music you need to sing.

Oh, and there is one more downside. What if you ever get sick of that style of music, or you find you can't pay the bills with it? I know that probably sounds out of the question, but it is actually a small crisis for a lot of adult singers right now. In college most singers study classical singing, and a lot of them fall in love with it and hope to become professional opera singers. The problem is, there aren't enough opera companies to support all of these opera singers, and what they learned is so specialized that they are often trapped by the technique. These adults then have to start over again with a new style - to learn to sing in a completely different way.

The solution to problem number one, no mentor, has a solution - the Internet! No matter what the style, you can find an online mentor or teacher who can tell you what you need to know. It might be a performer, a teacher, or a vocal coach, but there will be somebody to advise you on your path. But be super careful! I know of many cases where the person who looked like a mentor turned out to be a crook. A really good crook looks for somebody's passion, acts like they share the passion, and then takes their money and breaks their spirit. Do not give any self-professed teacher, coach, or agent any money unless you and your parents have done research. Look at the teacher's web presence and reviews. Talk to the teacher/coach/mentor on the phone or video chat. Compare what they are charging to what other teachers are charging. Ask about them in social networks. If it is a social network devoted to their kind of singing, it would be surprising if nobody has heard of them, but if that's the case, walk away.

Problem number two is more tricky because it will definitely slow you down. It will either slow you down now, as you create a more broad foundation for your singing by studying different styles, or it will slow you down when you are an adult and have to learn a new way. Here's what I recommend: find a teacher  who knows, loves, and respects your style, but also demands you get familiar with other styles at the same time. It's not just about the notes, language, or sound color. It's about the muscle development, mental coordination, breath management, and resonance habits. You give your brain and body the gift of demanding the flexibility of singing in different styles; you'll be giving yourself a huge gift down the road.

Here's an example of how that works in a different athletic art form; dance. Say there is this dancer who is crazy about hip-hop, and really, really good at it. She spends hours each day dancing, watching dancers, and researching moves (exactly like you do with singing). She becomes great! At age 23 she lands an audition with Bruno Mars' company for his next tour. The problem is, Bruno's dancers are also expected to tap and throw in some ballet moves. Is she good enough in tap and ballet to compete? No way - she'll be competing against dancers who have cross-trained in five or more dance styles their whole lives. The moral of the story for you as a singer is: if you want to be competitive, cross-train your voice.

Any and All Styles

I hear you - this is me! I could never choose. All singing is great. In fact, last weekend I sang with a rock band, next weekend I'm singing an alto solo from Handel's Messiah (classical singing), and the following weekend I'll be in a musical. Sometimes I sing alto, sometimes I sing soprano,  and occasionally I sing tenor. I even sang and acted the tenor lead in an operetta once. How is a girl to choose? Or better yet, do we have to choose?

The answer is that if you want to make your living as a singer, eventually you do have to choose, but maybe not yet. There are two main reasons you might want to wait to choose. 1) You can explore a variety of genres in college and see which brings you the most joy. 2) You will learn what your audience likes most to hear you sing, which might very well mean it would be your most dependable career choice and easiest path to follow.

After you pick a genre you can still stay really good in lots of different types of singing, but most of your focus needs to be on the one that you are identifying with as a professional pursuit.

Starting Down The Professional Singer Road - College or Other?

The key point to a career as a professional singer is to pick a goal and devote your study, free time, and career toward getting to that goal. And remember, life is in the journey, not the goal. Look for a college or university with an academic major that you are interested in. In other words, if you want to be a solo R&B singer, don't go to a choir college or school with only classical singers. Same with musical theater. If you want to be an opera singer, you are set for college; there are literally hundreds of colleges that would love to have you, but for other genres, you need to look a little harder.

Networking (also known as building community) is a huge part of this field. It starts in High School and is even more important in college. Find people with a passion for the same kind of music you have.

For managing your own career, a double major or minor in business with an emphasis in entrepreneurship is a great idea (this is what I did). You'll need a little bit of everything from bookkeeping to marketing in your chosen field. Make sure you get it in college.

Another great side-track to at least become familiar with in college is Audio Engineering. When you get to the point that you are in the recording booth laying down your tracks, understanding the power of the audio engineer will really help.

College isn't an option? Then you can put together the same types of things on your own. Take business classes in high school and continue after you graduate by studying free online classes. They are offered by many schools and are called MOOCs (Massive Open Online Courses). A MOOC has college level content without the price tag - they are free for anybody to take - but also without the degree at the end.

Find a mentor who can help you become a part-time independent voice teacher. The best way to learn is to teach.

Get a job at the places you'd like to perform at some day; it's great for learning the ropes and networking. It is also a chance to see if the performers at the venue actually have and enjoy the life you are considering as your goal.

After college, avoid getting stuck long-term in an office job thinking it will help pay the bills until you get on your feet. You'll find yourself stifled, exhausted, and without time to pursue your dream job. Instead take part time and freelance jobs so you can be free for auditions.

Becoming a professional singer and maintaining it as a career takes singular focus without compromise. If this is where your passion is, you will have an amazing but challenging journey.

Reality TV Singing Contests

Have you thought about auditioning for one of the reality TV shows? That seems really exciting, doesn't it? A short route to fame and spotlights. The experience for those singers seems to be amazing. Whenever I watch one, I think, "I could do that! They would love me!" But I know the dark side of that business, and you need to know about it too, so that you really use your head when making a decision to go for something so huge.

To get into this deeper with a voice teacher who has the same opinion as most voice teachers around the country, I talked with Alexis Lara O'Donahue of *Voices That Get Heard Studio*

Nancy: Alexis, have you ever had a high school or middle school student who wanted to do a reality show singing contest?

Alexis: Yes! Let's call her Linda, and she was 12 years old. She loved to sing, was active in school choir, and faithfully watched every reality show that featured singing. She saw kids, younger even than herself, becoming the hit of the night with their big songs, big voices, long held high notes, lots of vocal pyrotechnics and she knew she could do that easily, even though she'd had no formal voice instruction at that point. In truth she was gifted with wonderful pitch perception and a naturally beautiful voice that easily made her the star of her school. She wanted to know how to audition for those big TV reality shows and become a star.

Nancy: So when she came to you for voice lessons she was preparing to audition. What did she say?

Alexis: She introduced herself with "Hi, I'm Linda and I'm going to be a star." Okay! Now this may sound obnoxious, but truly, it wasn't. She was a very sweet and likable girl, truly blessed with a great deal of talent and a natural voice, and a decided flair for the dramatic. She saw no reason why her abilities shouldn't grant her stardom, and soon!

Nancy: So how did the lessons go?

Alexis: After a few sessions, Linda's natural voice abilities and pitch perception were strongly demonstrated, along with the fact that she had not yet learned to practice effectively because it all came so easily. We talked about the fact that she would only progress so far without learning how to learn, how to have an effective practice that protected her vocal instrument and grow into more challenging music as she developed.

Nancy: Were her parents thinking the same thing - that she should audition for a show?

Alexis: Her mom told me that she wanted to audition as soon as possible for those big network singing shows, and wanted my help in getting her ready. She wanted to know, did I think she had a chance to be picked for the show?

The truth is, with this girl's natural talent, flair, and strong charisma, added to her young age, I thought there was actually a very good chance she would be picked to sing on any of the shows. And I said NO to that whole idea.

Nancy: Wait, you thought she was good enough. That's what she wanted and it would have been good for your business. Why say no?

Alexis: Did I want to be known as the voice teacher who taught the next big star of 'Generic singing TV show"? NO!

Here are some of the reasons why:

1. Physical development of a child's voice

2. Complicated repertoire (including arias, heavy belting that are intended for adult, mature voices)

3. Pressure to perform when the show needs you that a child does not know how to navigate

4. Ability to rest when needed

5. Emotional safety so that a child's self-worth is not resting on winning a competition

6. Expectations to deliver a 'winning' performance to meet expectations of the competition and/or parents

Primarily it all comes down to these shows need ratings, and is diametrically opposed to the child's need for healthful vocal practices, including a choice of songs that are safe for a young, developing voice.

Nancy: Wow, that is really big-picture stuff. You are right; on the shows we only see a 3 minute documentary and a 3 minute performance. We don't see the price the child and family pays in hard work and money. And we don't see the hours of practice, preparation, and stress!

Alexis: Exactly! A child's voice is not an adult's voice. Children's voices are still developing, still growing, just like the rest of their bodies. Somehow, our popular culture seems to have forgotten that. Just as you would not expect a young person to lift a heavy load that would be appropriate for an adult, the developing voice is not up to handling the demands of vocal work that is suitable for a grown up. Full scale opera arias sung by a young child are often met with astonishment at how mature this singing prodigy sounds. The same goes for kids belting out a musical theatre song, hitting high notes full out, holding them forever. Wow! Listen to this amazing kid who "sounds like an adult!"

The truth is, many shows geared toward children have songs that, while very catchy to listen to, are actually written for an adult voice, and are written for a vocalist who understands the specific technique of speech like singing, or 'belting.' A young child hears, imitates, and sings. This is not going to be terrible if it is limited to some fun around the house, but bringing that song to the level of professional performance on TV is another matter entirely.

Nancy: Tell us what the problem is with young voices singing songs written for and performed by people who are ten or more years older?

Alexis: What children have to do with their voices to accomplish those "adult" sounds is, at best, not good for them, and at worst, permanently damaging. When you watch these kids sing, it may seem to sound great, but a trained voice instructor can often see the tight throat, and certainly hear, the constriction, as they push air out and force an unnaturally huge sound out. Muscles around the larynx can become overly stressed, and the harsh friction of pushed air over the vocal folds and the slamming together of the vocal folds can create inflammation that can escalate to calluses and nodules. Like math, it is not just getting the right answer; it is how you got to the answer. The same is the case for vocalists. The way you sing, the knowledge and intelligence of using your one and only vocal instrument, is important. When you add the intensity of public performing to this stress, you can have lasting damage.

Nancy: Why would anyone want to take those risks?

Alexis: Our culture rewards people for winning the gold medal. No one wins a competition because they are taking exquisite care of their voice. As adults, we can handle those expectations. Children are still learning who they are, and rely on adults to model healthy expectations. When a voice teacher is coaching a child to have an appropriate repertoire and to practice healthy vocal habits, and at the same time the child sees the rewards of ignoring that solid advice in order to have success on TV, whom does the child believe?

It is very important to realize that children born with a natural voice can often mimic pretty much anything they hear. I had the same experience as a child when I heard what turned out to be Sempre Libera from La Traviata on the radio. I could copy what I heard by 11 years old. I had no idea what I was doing or how I was

doing it. My mother asked me how I could do that. I didn't know, I just sang what I heard. This does NOT mean that the child understands vocal technique that will protect them under the pressures of performing live, on TV, going on a 'winners of star search' tour, with pressure and expectation to sound as good or better than their audition with every performance. If that child is tired, has a cold, or their throat is feeling sore, are they going to not perform when so much is riding on it?

Nancy: But what if the parent really stands by their kid, hires great coaches, and travels with them?

Alexis: Children want their parents to be proud of them, and what a gigantic emotional burden if they do not win, to feel they have failed in such a large and public venue.

Tolerating the risk of failure-which nowadays is not getting the top gold medal prize, requires some maturity, and is not an expectation that should rest on a child's shoulder. Certainly parents can help their child understand that their worth does not rest on "winning," but why put your talented fabulous child under this stress in the first place?

Nancy: Are you saying kids shouldn't be professional performers?

Alexis: The voice is an instrument that can give great joy to life when it is treated well and nurtured. Am I against children performing? No, actually, I am not. Like any other experience we guide our young people through, the difference is handling our adult expectations of the child. I performed very young, but only under the watchful eyes of my mother. As young as four years of age, I would sing at the drop of a hat, at home, at school, and in public anywhere. I sang in school shows and choirs. I sang all the TV show themes and commercial jingles. I could not stop singing. The difference is, I was never once forced or pushed to sing music that was truly physically out of my league. My mom was there, and while not a trained voice professional, definitely enforced healthy guidelines. She stopped playing music at dinner because I would sing (or dance if it was instrument) and not sit down at the table and eat properly. When we did a show together, she made sure I napped before show time, and once pulled me out of a show when the hours were getting too long for a nine year old. I was not always happy about that at the time, but as I grew up, I was very grateful for her caring about my long-term health for my developing body and my developing voice.

Nancy: Where did this leave Linda and her mom? Did they leave and find another voice teacher to help them get onto 'The Voice'?

Alexis: Happily, no, they didn't! I taught Linda for several years and she moved on to university studies with a major in music and drama. She has solid technique and a steadily growing repertoire of wonderful music in a variety of styles.

I am so glad they saw the value of protecting and healthfully developing Linda's lovely natural gift, into a strong voice, bringing her (and anyone who hears her) a lifetime of joy through gorgeous music, sung beautifully and intelligently.

Nancy: What advice do you have for teenage girls who are thinking about auditioning for reality shows right now?

Alexis: I ask you to please consider all the points I've talked about. Be a teenager, sing teenager songs, sing in school and your community, and sing with a voice teacher. Take time to build your skills and sing happily for a long time to come.

Nancy: Thank you, Alexis! You have given us a lot to think about. It is good to have insight into the demands and expectations of the television industry on the singers. I still think of how happy the singers are on TV and in interviews, but I also realize it is important to think about how few make it to the top, and to know how hard they've worked and what they've sacrificed to get there.

Next Steps

It's time to wrap it up. We've talked about so many things. Mostly we've talked about the best things to do, and how to get started doing them, if you want your life to be centered around singing. Have you gotten some good ideas for starting out? Do you have a better understanding of how singing fits in your life and how to achieve as much music as you'd like? I hope you do.

I want to say it again, you aren't required to stay in one of the *5 Perspectives.* You have every right to float between them or combine a couple. You are unique.

Think of *The Teen Girl's Singing Guide* as the preparation and travel guide for your journey. This book helps you create the map, but it doesn't take the journey for you. Along the way, you will run into roadblocks and detours. You'll get sidetracked down interesting paths, and at some point you will need to decide if you still want to reach the destination your map is taking you to or if instead you want a new destination.

We looked into your heart and your head to find your true feelings about singing. Then we thought about how much priority you should give to singing when you include your other interests. Thinking about these things is really important. It's true that in order to be happy in life you must follow your heart. Go back to Part 1 every once in awhile to see if you still feel the same and have the same destination in mind.

Part 2 was all about different ways to fit singing into your life right now. What are the things you should do in your life over the next few years to achieve your singing goals and get to your destination?

And finally we worked on creating the map to get you started toward school and career goals, knowing you are headed in the right direction. Doesn't it feel great to have some of the fog lifted around singing?

I know you have had some ideas already that you'd love to tell somebody about, and I hope you will. Get your family involved with the take-away you have from this book. Talk to your friends or other music kids in your school to build community and support as you start on your journey.

Reach out to experts to learn more; people who are passionate about their field love it when teens want to learn more from them. And reach out to me on Instagram or through my website. I would LOVE to hear from you!

Finally, I'd like to leave you with some great advice about how to move forward:

> *Focus takes a lot of brainpower, so focusing on one goal at a time when learning will help diminish burnout. Set goals with your teacher (or your family) as to what you want to accomplish. Work at accomplishing smaller, stepping-stone goals to achieve the ultimate goal.*
>
> *Six-Word Lessons for Exceptional Music Lessons by Sally Palmer*

This book is also available as an audiobook on Audible.com and as a Kindle book.

Resources

Instagram.com/theteengirlssinging

Nancy Bos Voice Studio on Facebook @StudioBos101

Diana Allan
Empowering performers to excel! www.musicpeakperformance.com

Alexis O'Donahue   Voices that get heard
voicesthatgetheard.com

Sally Palmer
Six Word Lessons for Exceptional Music Lessons
sallylpalmer.weebly.com/book.html

Valerie White Williams
Vocal Splendor Studios vocalsplendor.com
YouTube.com//user/vocalsplendor

About The Author

Nancy Bos is a speaker, writer, podcaster (Every Sing podcast), vocologist, and voice coach. She has maintained an independent singing studio since 1995. She has served as adjunct faculty at Cornish College of the Arts, Seattle Pacific University, and is affiliated with Bellevue College. She is the author of *Singing 101: Vocal Basics and Fundamental Singing Skills for All Styles and Abilities* and co-author of *Singing Through Change: Women's Voices in Midlife, Menopause, and Beyond*. Nancy has given many master classes and presentations, which include popular contemporary singing styles, pedagogy for transgender singers, vocal acoustics, and music theater. Her students perform at major venues in all parts of the US.

Nancy has worked in the recording industry, film, and theater. A versatile performer, she has been the mezzo soprano soloist for music tours of Peru, Romania, and southern Europe, belted out musical theater character roles, and sung in bluegrass and rock concerts. She plays bass, keyboards, and even works as a voice over artist.

Nancy serves on the board of the Voice and Speech Trainers Association, and is a former Vice President for the National Association of Teachers of Singing. She is a Distinguished Voice Professional through NYSTA and a member of the Recording Academy. Nancy was raised in Sioux Falls, SD and received her undergraduate degree from Luther College, Decorah, Iowa.

These pages are for you.

Write about your passion for singing and write about your journey to achieving your dreams!

Made in the USA
Las Vegas, NV
11 April 2024

88545202R00085